the little book of
MODERN
WITCHCRAFT

Published in 2023 by OH!
An Imprint of Welbeck Non-Fiction Limited, part of Welbeck Publishing Group.
Offices in: London – 20 Mortimer Street, London W1T 3JW
and Sydney – Level 17, 207 Kent St, Sydney NSW 2000 Australia
www.welbeckpublishing.com

Compilation text copyrght © Welbeck Non-Fiction Limited 2023
Design © Welbeck Non-Fiction Limited 2023

Disclaimer:
This book and the information contained herein are for general educational
and entertainment use only. The contents are not claimed to be exhaustive,
and the book is sold on the understanding that neither the publishers nor the
author are thereby engaged in rendering any kind of professional services.
Users are encouraged to confirm the information contained herein with
other sources and review the information carefully with their appropriate,
qualified service providers. Neither the publishers nor the author shall have
any responsibility to any person or entity regarding any loss or damage
whatsoever, direct or indirect, consequential, special or exemplary, caused
or alleged to be caused, by the use or misuse of information contained in
this book.

All rights reserved. No part of this publication may be reproduced, stored
in a retrieval system, or transmitted in any form or by any means (including
electronic, mechanical, photocopying, recording, or otherwise) without prior
written permission from the publisher.

ISBN 978-1-80069-531-3

Editorial consultant: Katalin Patnaik
Editorial: Victoria Denne
Project manager: Russell Porter
Production: Jess Brisley

A CIP catalogue record for this book is available from the British Library

Printed in China

10 9 8 7 6 5 4 3 2 1

the little book of
MODERN WITCHCRAFT

katalin patnaik

CONTENTS

INTRODUCTION

Witchcraft can simply be described as harnessing the energy of the universe and using it with the power of the mind to influence our lives in a positive way.

Modern witchcraft is about being in tune with our natural resources and using them, through simple spells often including the lighting of candles, meditation, crystals, and other rituals connected to Pagan origins, to mystically satisfy our spiritual desires.

There are many traditions that could be catalogued as modern witchcraft. Some of these are Neo-paganism, Wicca, and the branches that sprout from them, like Gardnerian Wicca, Icelandic witchcraft, Asatru, Thursatru, Hellenism, Kemetism, and others.

For the sake of simplicity, we will discuss Eclectic Wicca in this book.

Gardner, a well-travelled,
retired civil servant with a great
interest in anthropology and
archaeology, based this new
religion on Freemasonry practices,
Hermeticism, Aleister Crowley's
teachings, ceremonial magic, and
the practices of indigenous people
of the Malay Archipelago.

He developed its theological
structure and rituals in the
1940s, and began to popularize
Wicca in existing covens and
occultist publications.

Unlike Christianity, Wicca doesn't have a central head of religion, or sacred scriptures. The closest thing to commandments that Gardner left behind is called the Wiccan Rede.

The word "rede" is Middle-English for advice, and is regarded as a guideline only, not as a hard-set rule or dogma.

The Wiccan Rede:
An, it harm none, do what ye will.

It means, *if it harms none, do what you want.* This, of course, is up to the individual's interpretation and morality, based on each situation one finds oneself.

an, it HARM
NONE,
do WHAT
YE WILL

Thanks to its decentralized nature, Wicca is still an evolving religion with countless traditions branching out from it, allowing its followers to choose the parts they truly resonate with. Because of this, some traditions might even be contradictory to each other in their teachings. What unites them, however, is their reverence for nature and universal balance.

The two most distinguishable groups of Wiccans are the followers of British Traditional Wicca, and Eclectic Wiccans.

BRITISH traditional WICCA

British Traditional Wicca is a strict denomination that requires initiation of its disciples into covens, along with secrecy about its practices.

It means only a witch can make a witch, and one can't just become a British Traditional Wiccan on a whim.

ECLECTIC WICCA

Eclectic Wicca is a more relaxed path that can be practiced in covens or solitarily as well. It doesn't require formal initiation or secrecy from its followers.

For Wiccans, the central figures of worship are the Triple Goddess and the Horned God (see Chapter 2).

Wiccans honour balance in duality, and the wholeness that is created by the union of the two archetypes.

Although the word "witch" has a female sound to it, witchcraft is for all genders. Male practitioners often refer to themselves as witches as well.

Other words you might come across are warlock and wizard, although the former might have a negative connotation to some.

CHAPTER

ETHICS

While witchcraft has no commandments and treatises on how to be a good person, its practitioners certainly strive to be good.

being
GOOD

What "being good" means, however, and how it manifests in one's actions, will differ from person to person, situation to situation.

All kinds of witchcraft are very practical systems. While other religions have well established rules, witches measure the rightness of their actions by the outcomes and consequences they bring.

They strive for:

- **balance**
- **harmony**
- **justice**
- **peace**

Witches are careful of how they use Earth's resources. They are aware of the environment's struggles, and they do their part to stop things from getting worse.

This can mean:

- responsible, mindful consumption

- attending protests against climate change

- hexing illegal wood cutters or wildlife smugglers

Can witches hex, then?

Many witches feel passionate about environmental and social issues, and use their talents to stop the harm that is being done to the environment or to marginalized people around the world.

Witches have teamed up many times in history to hex and curse political figures, leaders, monarchs and dictators.

If it saves others from harm, then offensive magic might be justified.

To quote Dietrich Bonhoeffer:

"Silence in the face of evil is itself evil."

DIETRICH BONHOEFFER

If you don't know what kind of curses are possible, how could you break them, or protect yourself and your loved ones?

It is worth looking into offensive magic, even if only to better prepare yourself against it.

As the saying goes:

"One who
cannot
curse,
cannot cure."

Use your own moral judgement for what kind of spells you perform, but before starting anything, consider the consequences of your actions.

It is a good idea to establish your beliefs about divine justice, karma, the rule of three, and other such concepts in advance.

You might also wish to use a divination tool to find out what kind of outcome the spell might bring, both short term, long term, and for your soul.

CHAPTER

WORKING
with GODS

Most witches, no matter which tradition they belong to, are polytheistic – believing in more than one god, or deity – but you can also be an atheistic witch, not believing in any god.

Whilst there is no obligation to worship any god, or to work with any spirit, it can certainly help.

Wicca can be viewed both as a duotheistic and henotheistic religion at the same time.

Dualism is the belief in two gods, which often oppose each other, ruling the universe, whilst henotheism does not deny the existence, or possible existence, of other gods or deities.

The two main deities are the Triple Goddess, whose symbol is shown above, and the Horned God, whose symbol is shown below.

The Triple Goddess is the archetypal female force, therefore her followers can work with Goddesses Kali, Hecate or Freyja, too.

Witches usually view these individual goddesses as manifestations of the Triple Goddess. Because they are parts of, or manifestations of, the main Goddess, worshipers can establish a more personal relationship with them.

Wiccans see deities in everything, especially nature. They understand that everything is interconnected; everything is part of the divine.

Every tree, every animal, every place has a spirit inhabiting it, and Wiccans regard that spirit with great respect.

They also believe that the God and Goddess are present in us humans.

We are part of the divine, and therefore we are divine as well. We need to respect that divinity in ourselves, and in our fellow humans.

Accepting this divinity also makes it possible to form a healthier relationship with spirits and deities than is usually seen in monotheistic religions.

Witches have a trusting, intimate relationship with gods and goddesses. Deities can be guides, parent figures, siblings, even lovers to a witch.

Witches take time to build relationships to their chosen deities, and call on them when they need them, be it for a spell, or for a rant about the traffic jam they are stuck in.

The same deity can show themselves in different ways to different people.

The Goddess Kali can show herself as a ruthless warrior one needs to be scared of, or as a benevolent, although strict mother figure who fiercely protects her people.

How a deity appears to someone always comes down to what the deity feels a practitioner needs.

If you feel drawn to a deity, the first thing to do is to read up on them. Some deities are OK to work with for anyone, but some are exclusive to certain groups of people, based on race, culture or location.

Worshipping closed deities will cause upset in that community, and will be perceived as appropriation.

If you find out the deity you like is exclusive to a certain group of people, you need to respectfully step back and look for an alternative.

Some deities of living traditions need rituals to be carried out in a certain way, and doing them wrong could cause upset to their followers, and may mean you are rejected by the deity.

REVIVED RELIGIONS

In general, revived religions are considered open to anyone.

Greek, Roman, Norse and Egyptian deities are safe to worship, because these religions have died out, meaning there is no danger of appropriating someone's living culture.

LIVING RELIGIONS

Living religions, like Buddhism or Hinduism, have certain rules that need to be respected.

They are generally open to anyone to join, but not following the rules will be regarded as disrespectful, and may result in being rejected by the god or goddess you are trying to work with.

CLOSED RELIGIONS

Closed religions are those that have requested to be off-limits to outsiders who were not born into them. This is to protect the religion and culture that might be in decline.

Some of the closed religions are

- Hoodoo
- Vodou
- Santería
- Brujería

Many people worship deities from different cultures. It is up to you whether you want to stick with one pantheon, or pick deities you like from around the world. Ultimately, however, it will be the deity's choice whether they want to work with you.

There are certain covens that require their members to worship one certain group of deities, while others welcome variety. See what suits you best when looking for community on your journey.

Some deities have a bad reputation –
deities associated with Death and the
Underworld may be mistakenly viewed
as evil, equal to Christianity's Satan.

Always do your own research, and
you will see that, for example, Hades
is one of the most understanding,
patient and forgiving gods, who can
teach a great deal about transformation,
mourning, acceptance and letting go.

Always remember:

- Witches do not fear deities – unless a practitioner has done something truly disrespectful towards their god.

- Witches don't expect deities to solve their problems for them, and they never demand anything from them, or try to bribe them.

On the contrary, witches:

- Ask the deities to lend them power to overcome problems on their own, and they make offerings out of love and gratitiude.

- Do the mundane work, and ask for the deities' help only for mental and spiritual strength to get on with it.

Communicating with deities and spirits can be done in many ways, even if you're not a psychic.

Asking your deity to appear in a dream is one of the most popular ways of finding out what they want from you. Other methods are through divination, for example getting a tarot or rune reading done, or looking out for signs throughout the day.

As an example, the Norse god Loki is famous for messing with electronic items – if you have frequent, unexplained troubles with your electronics, it might be him trying to catch your attention, especially if you've been thinking about him lately.

talking to
DEITIES

Talking to deities and
other spirits is easier than
it may appear.

- Settle down, focus your intention on the deity you want to send a message to, and say what you want, either out loud or in your head.

- Then, and this is the tricky part: listen for an answer.

  It may come in many forms; a feeling, a thought, a sensation of someone standing behind you or touching your shoulder.

- You need to be assertive, and separate your own thoughts and biases from what comes from a spirit.

- Be ready to hear uncomfortable truths and opinions that are different to your own.

Something that all of them disapprove of, however, is disrespect.

As long as you worship them from a pure heart, and give them the respect they deserve, you should be alright. They understand that we all have different abilities and circumstances, both physically and financially.

CHAPTER

FESTIVALS
and sabbaths

the SUN
and the MOON

Witches and Pagans celebrate many festivals that are tied to the Sun's and the Moon's movement across the sky.

The festivals of the Sun are called Sabbats, and the celebrations tied to the Moon are called Esbats.

SABBATS

Sabbats are solar festivals that are usually celebrated with friends, the whole coven, or an even bigger crowd, depending on what you have access to.

There are eight Sabbats in a year: the two equinoxes, the two solstices, and four seasonal festivals that are placed halfway in between these.

ESBATS

Esbats are more personal, and aren't grandiose festivals that would bring crowds together. They are more suited for coven gatherings, and doing magic on a personal level.

It may sound strange, but these festivals are celebrated at different times depending on whether you live in the Northern or the Southern hemisphere.

remember:

These festivals are tied to nature and the cycle of life. Celebrating the harvest festival of Lughnasadh when spring just sprang in Australia wouldn't make sense.

SAMHAIN, the FESTIVAL of the ANCESTORS

The witches' new year: Halloween.

It is dear to many witches, not only because dressing up in witchy attires is acceptable in public, but because this is the festival where they honour the ancestors.

This is the time of the year when the veil between the worlds is the thinnest, and communication with the other side is the easiest.

Wiccans celebrate and commune with their ancestors, and show gratitude for new additions to their lives – people and opportunities alike.

Carving Jack-o'-Lanterns to keep negative spirits away and offering food to our spirit family are important parts of this beloved festival.

Northern Hemisphere:
31 October

Southern Hemisphere:
30 April

YULE,
the FESTIVAL of
RETURNING
LIGHT

Yule falls on the Winter Solstice.

This is the pagan originator of Christmas. Many witches celebrate both, or add pagan elements to their family's Christmas celebrations; you don't have to forego rituals from the religion you belonged to before.

If you do decide to celebrate both, try getting a potted Christmas tree as a way of showing love and respect to nature, and keep it for next year if you can.

It is traditional that when nature is asleep, and everything looks bleak, people bring evergreens into the house to lighten the darkness.

Mistletoe symbolizes fertility, holly gives protection, and ivy reminds us that life does endure, despite all hardships.

Witches light candles to celebrate the rebirth of the Sun, and turn inwards to descend into the deepest depths of their souls to bring back wisdom, and to plant the seeds of personal growth.

Northern Hemisphere:
20–22 December

Southern Hemisphere:
20–21 June

IMBOLC, the FESTIVAL of NEW LIFE and the FEAST of BRIGID

Imbolc is the first festival of the calendar year (in the Northern hemisphere at least).

It celebrates the arrival of new life after the long winter. Sheep give birth to their young around this time, and new leaves start to appear on plants, too.

The festival is dedicated to the goddess Brigid, patron of healing, new life, poetry and fire.

Wiccan women prepare a brideog, an effigy of the goddess made from sheaves of wheat on the previous day, and place her in a basket overnight to welcome her in.

On Imbolc, women perform rituals, and men bring gifts to the Goddess.

The brideog is then used to confess one's wishes and desires to the Goddess, in the hopes of them being granted.

Northern Hemisphere:
1–2 February

Southern Hemisphere:
1 August

OSTARA, the FESTIVAL of FERTILITY and RENEWAL

Ostara falls on the Spring Equinox – one of the two times a year when day and night are the same length. This is the pagan originator of Easter.

The festival's symbols are all to do with fertility and growth. In fact, one of the Goddess Ostara's main symbols is a hare, an animal that is known to reproduce prolifically – and this is thought to be where the Easter bunny comes from.

On Ostara, witches decorate hollowed-out eggs and fill them with whispered wishes they'd like to grow into reality by summer.

These eggs are then hung in the sacred space on a found (never a cut) branch from a tree, to give a visual reminder of the goals the witch is working towards.

Ostara is a good time to start new projects, or to pray for fertility in one's life.

Northern Hemisphere:
19–21 March

Southern Hemisphere:
21–23 September

BELTANE, the FESTIVAL of the GREEN MAN

Beltane invites in summer.

Wiccans celebrate the Green Man, a form of the Horned God, joining the Goddess by her side.

In nature, masculine and feminine energies are equal at this time, and that provides auspicious energy for starting new partnerships.

This is the time for handfasting ceremonies, having consensual fun, feasting, and erecting the May Pole to dance around.

Witches light bonfires, or candles if they are celebrating indoors, to get purified by the smoke, and to make promises and vows for the coming year.

Many people visit ancient, sacred wells, or leave out offerings for the faerie folk, because just like at Samhain, the veil between our worlds is very thin in this period.

Northern Hemisphere:
1 May

Southern Hemisphere:
31 October–1 November

LITHA,
the SUMMER
SOLSTICE

Litha falls on the Summer Solstice, the longest day of the year.

It celebrates the Sun god, the Oak King's height of power. Wiccans hold feasts and handfasting ceremonies at this time to celebrate the warm days of summer.

It is a custom to light bonfires at Litha to protect the autumn harvest.

Herbs picked on this day are the most potent, so make sure to harvest and process whatever is available to you. Even if you don't have a herb garden, go out into nature and enjoy the abundance.

Plucking the flowers and making elderflower syrup, or spreading stingingnettle leaves to dry for making herbal tea, can all be part of how you celebrate Litha.

Many pagans visit Stonehenge on this day, to see the Sun rise and set between the stones. In recent years, an online live stream has been set up that follows the Sun's movement all day.

Northern Hemisphere:
20–21 June

Southern Hemisphere:
21–22 December

LUGHNASADH, the HARVEST FESTIVAL

On this day, Wiccans celebrate the harvest of crops that are going to be brought in this season.

Many places hold harvest festivals, too, like people have been doing for centuries.

The bread-blessing festival, Lammas, is on the same day, and many witches celebrate the two together by baking a loaf and placing it on their altar for the gods to bless, before eating it for dinner.

Witches make dolls out of corn leaves to represent the harvest, and place them on their altars to show gratitude for what they have.

This is a good time to think about inequality in society, and work for a better future for all.

This is also the time to practice your skills, too, be it arts, sports, or anything you are good at.

There are often competitions held by covens on this day, to commemorate the many talents of the god Lugh.

Northern Hemisphere:
1 August

Southern Hemisphere:
1 February

MABON,
the AUTUMN
EQUINOX

The last festival of the Wiccan year is Mabon, when the day and the night are equal, and when the nights start to get longer.

Mabon commemorates the second harvest, the time fruits like apples and grapes are brought in.

Witches slice apples horizontally, to reveal the five-pointed star that surrounds the seeds within.

They eat apples to remind themselves of the blessings they have received from the Goddess, and to remember their magical place in the universe, and their responsibilities as witches.

Northern Hemisphere:
21–22 September

Southern Hemisphere:
21–22 March

The turning of the seasons
is beautifully illustrated
in the symbolic story of birth,
death and rebirth of the
solar God.

On Yule, the Goddess gives birth to the Star Child, causing the days to get longer. The Star Child will grow into a young man by Ostara, and then father the next Star Child with the Maiden aspect of the Goddess.

By Mabon, the Mother aspect of the Goddess is in her third trimester, and the God begins his descent into the Underworld, or to the Summerlands, as an old man.

On Samhain, the Crone aspect of the Goddess helps the God cross over to the Summerlands, making way for the new Star Child to be born on Yule.

To celebrate each festival, decorate your altar (see page 114) with matching items, and think about how you can make the world a better place, even if it is only for your immediate surroundings.

Making your own dollies and picking your own decorations from nature walks makes magic more personal, but store-bought things will work just as well.

A witch is always practical: use whatever is available to you.

CHAPTER

4

COMMUNITY

COVENS

Back in the day, it could be hard to find a coven, or any fellow witches at all.

Thankfully, those days are over.

There are occult shops where you could ask for information about local covens, or you could find them on the internet and social media sites.

Even if you live in a really conservative area, you will still be able to join online forums and Zoom Esbats.

Joining a coven, or just having friends who share your practice, is really beneficial. You can only learn so much from books; interacting and practicing with fellow Wiccans can teach you more, faster.

The written word can sometimes be confusing, too. Being able to talk to someone and clear your doubts helps with your confidence, which, in turn, increases the impact of your spells.

You are allowed to be choosy when picking a coven. If you feel one doesn't align with your core beliefs, you can move on.

Never compromise your ethics for anyone.

Remember, just because a group of people says something is right, it doesn't necessarily mean it is.

Joining a coven, or having fellow witch friends, is also useful when performing spells. Spells performed by groups of people are exponentially stronger than those performed alone. Especially when embarking on this journey, you might have experiences that are hard to believe. It is reassuring to hear others experiencing the same thing.

Validation in the early stages of practicing witchcraft is beneficial. People who have been practicing longer can tell you if you are way off-track in something, too.

Practicing witchcraft means continuous work on yourself; you need to be ready to hear constructive criticism, too.

That said, you may encounter people who talk down to you from their high horses, stating that only their way is right.

The difference between good advice and bad is the intention. In any case, hear all criticism, take what is useful, and leave the rest.

CHAPTER

5

PRACTICING WITCHCRAFT

TOOLS
you will need

The athame, or a ritual dagger, is a versatile tool that draws and directs energy during rituals. It can be used for casting the sacred circle, or harvesting herbs and other plants for magical purposes, among many other things.

Some witches prefer to keep a separate knife for actual cutting of physical things, which is called a boline. It is up to you which way you prefer to do it.

ATHAME

An athame usually has a black hilt, and is roughly as long as your hand. You can forge your own, buy one online, or use a simple kitchen knife – just keep it separate from your other knives.

An athame should only be used for ritual purposes.

BOLINE

A boline on the other hand is not used in rituals. It usually has a white hilt, and is used for actual cutting, like harvesting herbs, shaping a branch into a wand, or preparing magical food.

WAND

The wand has a similar role to the athame. It is used for casting the circle, drawing sigils into the air and the ground, and directing energy into a focus point.

It is traditionally made of wood, but you can buy wands that are made of crystals, glass, or metal as well.

BELL

A bell is used for cleansing the energies in your surroundings, and to announce to the God and Goddess that a magical act is going to commence. It acts as a doorbell to the deities, and lets them know you request their attention.

You'll often find bells or chimes above entries to shops or homes, to keep out negative energy.

BROOM or BESOM

A broom or besom is used to energetically cleanse the space before casting the sacred circle, but after a physical cleansing by regular, mundane tools. After the ritual, dismissing the circle with the broom is an effective way to prevent residual energy lingering behind, especially after banishing rituals. It is usually made of a tree's branches, but you can use a regular broom, too. Just make sure it is brand new, and has a wooden handle.

CUP

A cup is used to offer drinks to the gods, hold water or other liquids for rituals, or be passed around the members of the coven in rituals and celebrations of sharing mead or ale.

It is traditionally made of silver, but any metal, glass, ceramic or wooden cup will do.

Be aware that certain drinks, such as alcohol or lemonade, can corrode some metals and make your drink toxic.

PENTACLE

A pentacle is used in rituals to represent Earth, and to charge tools and ingredients before you use them.

Many witches wear pentacle necklaces, too.

CAULDRON

A cauldron is a fireproof vessel that is used for fire rituals, holding incense and candles, and preparing ointments and salves. You could buy it online, or use a regular cooking vessel.

INCENSE

The smoke of incenses can be used as an offering to the deities, or as a tool to give additional potency to your spells. Nag champa incense sticks are great to get you started, but gradually expand your collection, and even make your own loose incense.

If for any reason you can't burn incense, you may consider using essential oils, but fragrances are not crucial to witchcraft, so you can leave this out altogether.

remember:

Never use magical tools
for mundane purposes.

These need to be kept
separately, to protect
their energy.

creating an
ALTAR

An altar is a sacred place where you keep your magical items.

You don't need to have a dedicated room, or a huge shrine for it; in fact, you can fit it in a small box, if you need to practice discreetly, or if you don't have much space in your home.

Always keep things practical.

Pick a place that is not going to be disturbed in your everyday life. A place that's not in anyone's way, where children or pets won't knock over anything, and where nothing can catch fire from the candles.

Ideally, your altar shouldn't be in your bedroom, but if you have no other option, make sure it can be covered when you are sleeping, out of respect.

You may want to cover it when you engage in anything sexual, too, unless you are doing sex magic.

Your altar has three main functions.

- It is a sacred space where you focus your intention on magic and worship.

- It can hold the statues of deities you work with, along with the things you offer to them.

- It can also house everything that is connected to your practice: an astrological chart, your tarot deck, your athame, crystals, books, your grimoire, and other magical items.

Another function of the altar is to hold ingredients of your spells until the spell is active.

Your altar can also serve as a spell in itself. Taking advantage of it as a type of vision board, you can decorate it with things that help you focus on your intent.

DIVINATION and OTHER DISCIPLINES

It is not mandatory to learn anything extra to add to your practice, but it is useful.

It's also fun to learn different disciplines, and it makes spellcasting and working with spirits easier.

TAROT

Many witches learn to read tarot, because it is the most direct and nuanced way of divination.

Don't be intimidated by the 78 cards; learning them only takes dedication and practice.

LENORMAND and KIPPER CARDS

Other card systems you could consider learning are Lenormand and Kipper cards, both of which have gained a lot of popularity in recent years.

RUNES

Runes are excellent tools of divination as well. Creating your own rune kit is a magical act in itself, and speeds up your learning, as opposed to buying your kit ready-made.

These ancient letters are great for communicating with the spirit world.

NUMEROLOGY

Numerology can help a great deal in decision-making and gauging someone's personality.

It is also helpful when you choose your witch name, by which you will be known in your coven.

seven magical
TIPS

1 Writing your own spells will give
   them more power and positive
   results because you are putting your
   intention into the spell.

2 It is advisable to keep a spell
   book (or Book of Shadows, as
   it is sometimes called) to write
   notes about the spells for future
   reference.

3 You may just write down the appropriate words required for the type of spell you are making, or you can write down the words in rhyme.

4 Concentrate on the wording of your spell before you start so that you put your full intention into your spell.

5 Never use a candle that has been lit before.

6 Snuff the candle out, or if you blow it out, ensure that it goes out and stays out.

7 Never leave a burning candle unattended.

ASTROLOGY

Astrology is really helpful to time your spells, and to prepare people's charts to get to know them better. A good astrological chart reveals areas where one is strong, and where one needs more improvement. It is therefore a great tool for self-help.

HERBOLOGY

Herbology complements witchcraft well. Using herbs for spells, and to heal physical and emotional wounds, is often how people define witches.

the FIVE ELEMENTS

In witchcraft, the five elements are often used to enhance spells, and to cast a magic circle.

The elements are Air, Fire, Earth, Water and Spirit (or Ether), and they are symbolized by the pentagram.

AIR

Air is associated with the cardinal direction of east, the colour yellow, with Swords or Wands in tarot (depending on the tradition), and with the concept of communication and intellect.

Its symbols for spells and your altar are: incense, feathers, wind chimes, pens, your athame or wand.

FIRE

Fire is associated with the cardinal direction of south, the colour red, with Swords or Wands in tarot (depending on the tradition), and with the concept of passion and activity.

Its symbols for spells and your altar are: candles or oil lamps, lizards, the Sun, your athame or wand.

WATER

Water is associated with the cardinal direction of west, the colour blue, with Cups in tarot, and with the concept of emotions and intuition.

Its symbols for spells and your altar are: cups, fishes and water creatures, the Moon.

EARTH

Earth is associated with the cardinal direction of north, the colour green, with Pentacles in tarot, and with the concept of fertility and grounding.

Its symbols for spells and your altar are: stones, coins, plants, a pentacle.

SPIRIT

Spirit is above and in the middle. It is associated with the colour purple, with the Major Arcana in tarot, and with the concept of spirituality and transformation.

Its symbols for spells and your altar are: crystals and statues of deities.

the SACRED CIRCLE

Using the five elements, together with blessed water and salt, you cast the sacred circle, sometimes called the magic circle, to consecrate the space you are about to do something magical in.

Drawing a sacred circle gives extra power to your practice, be it spells or other magical acts, and it provides protection against negative energies and entities that might try to latch on to you.

You don't have to cast a circle for every spell. It's usually for bigger rituals only, but it is entirely up to you whether you want to make one or not.

When you are a beginner, it is advisable to do it, if only for the practice of noticing the shifting energies.

Before anything, you need to find a place to practice magic. It could be indoors or outdoors, it doesn't matter.

The only requirement is that it should give you privacy long enough to perform your ritual.

Cleanse yourself and this place in the physical realm first. Take a shower, put on clean clothes, then tidy up the space, hoover or mop the floor.

Concentrate on getting rid of any negative energy that might linger there, and without touching the floor, sweep the place with your besom. This makes the place and your mind ready for the ritual.

After tidying, bless the place with positive, conductive energy, and invite any deities you want to work with. You are now ready to cast your circle.

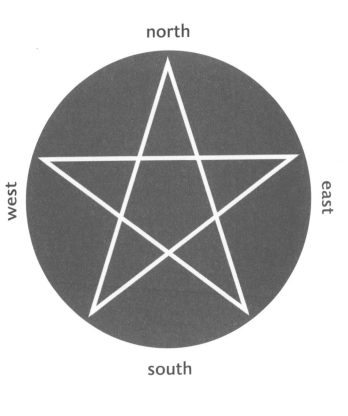

A sacred circle is usually 9 feet in diameter, but practicality overrides tradition, as always. If you don't have space, cast a circle that is just big enough for you and your ingredients.

Alternatively, consider the whole room as a circle and, when casting, sprinkle the salty water on the walls in the same manner you'd draw the circle.

If you are outdoors, don't use salty water, as it may harm the environment – it makes soil infertile, and kills snails and slugs.

You could create a mental circle, draw one in the soil with your athame or wand, or make one with twigs or rocks, using whatever is around you.

Be mindful of what you use, and don't harm anything by doing so.

When your space is ready, mark the elements in their directions with corresponding candles or tokens. For example, to mark Air/East, you could use a yellow candle, or a feather, and so on.

Place these items in the corresponding directions, with Spirit in the middle of the circle.

Once you have marked the directions, you will need blessed water and salt.

To make blessed water, take a bowl, fill it with water, hold it in both hands, and send your intention through your hands into the water.

Concentrate on cleansing and charging it with positive, protective energy. When this is done, mix salt into it.

Say out loud or in your head:

"I cleanse and bless this water and salt in the name of the Goddess. May they cleanse and protect my ritual."

Now, using your athame or a wand, draw an actual circle with the salt water, or scatter it in a circle around you, moving clockwise, with you standing in the middle. Start at East, and move towards South, West, North, and finally arrive back where you started.

Circles are drawn clockwise, or deosil – the way the Sun moves. This is considered to be an auspicious direction in most cultures. While casting, concentrate on inviting in divine energy, asking for protection. Nothing can cross this circle that you haven't invited in. You are protected.

Once the circle is drawn, do not leave it until you are finished with your ritual, as this will disturb the circle and weaken it.

If you need to leave the circle for any reason, use the same tool you made the circle with, and make an opening, a door in the East, where you can leave, or let someone in.

When you are settled, close this door by connecting the line of the circle with the salt water again.

When you are done with your ritual and you don't need the circle anymore, you have to release, or close it. This is done by giving gratitude to the elements and the deities that helped you in your ritual, and casting the circle anti-clockwise, starting with East and moving towards North.

When you're finished, wipe up the salty water in the same fashion, and sweep the space with your besom.

CHAPTER

preparation of

SPELL-
CASTING

SPELL-CASTING

Spells work with sympathetic magic – you act out in a magical way what you want to happen, and offer the Universe or your deities tokens that represent your goal.

consider
TIMING

You can perform any spell at any time, but it is beneficial to harness the power of the Moon cycle, the days of the week, and the time of the day.

WAXING MOON

A waxing, growing Moon is great for spells that invite in any type of energy: money, love, health, etc.

WANING MOON

A waning, shrinking Moon is great for releasing energy: cutting cords, letting go of grief or heartache, etc.

the FULL MOON

The Full Moon is the best time to prepare Moon water, which is a blessed water charged with the power of the Moon that you can use in rituals and for cleansing your home and tools. The Full Moon is also the time for celebrations, giving gratitude, or gathering for Esbats.

the NEW MOON

The New Moon is the time you initiate new beginnings, new projects, and invite new people into your life.

157

HOURS and PLANETS

Each daylight hour is ruled by a planet, which can influence your spell by focusing it to a specfic time. This sequence of associated hours and planets is known as the Chaldean order (see pages 162–163).

Each planet is associated with specific influences and energies:

- **the Sun** – harness the sun's strongest energy at sunrise, noon and sunset.

- **the Moon** – especially strong at the time of a New or Full Moon.

- **Mercury** – associated with healing, and particularly strong on Wednesdays.

- **Venus** – the Roman goddess of love.

- **Mars** – good times for spells that require action and activity.

- **Jupiter** – strong associations with travel, learning and spirituality.

- **Saturn** – a useful planet for when wisdom is needed.

Each day of the week is associated with a specific energy:

- **Sunday** is the day of the Sun, and it carries masculine energies.

- **Monday** is the day of the Moon, and it carries feminine energies.

- **Tuesday** is the day of Tyr, the Norse god of war, negotiation and justice.

- **Wednesday** is the day of Odin, the Norse god of war, magic and poetry.

- **Thursday** is the day of Thor, the Norse god of thunder, the sky and agriculture.

- **Friday** is the day of Freya, the Norse Goddess of war, the dead, love and fertility.

- **Saturday** is the day of Loki, the Norse trickster, god of mischief and transformation.

HOUR	SUN	MON	TUE
01.00	Sun	Moon	Mars
02.00	Venus	Saturn	Sun
03.00	Mercury	Jupiter	Venus
04.00	Moon	Mars	Mercury
05.00	Saturn	Sun	Moon
06.00	Jupiter	Venus	Saturn
07.00	Mars	Mercury	Jupiter
08.00	Sun	Moon	Mars
09.00	Venus	Saturn	Sun
10.00	Mercury	Jupiter	Venus
11.00	Moon	Mars	Mercury
12.00	Saturn	Sun	Moon
13.00	Jupiter	Venus	Saturn
14.00	Mars	Mercury	Jupiter
15.00	Sun	Moon	Mars
16.00	Venus	Saturn	Sun
17.00	Mercury	Jupiter	Venus
18.00	Moon	Mars	Mercury
19.00	Saturn	Sun	Moon
20.00	Jupiter	Venus	Saturn
21.00	Mars	Mercury	Jupiter
22.00	Sun	Moon	Mars
23.00	Venus	Saturn	Sun
24.00	Mercury	Jupiter	Venus

the hour and the day

WED	THU	FRI	SAT
Mercury	Jupiter	Venus	Saturn
Moon	Mars	Mercury	Jupiter
Saturn	Sun	Moon	Mars
Jupiter	Venus	Saturn	Sun
Mars	Mercury	Jupiter	Venus
Sun	Moon	Mars	Mercury
Venus	Saturn	Sun	Moon
Mercury	Jupiter	Venus	Saturn
Moon	Mars	Mercury	Jupiter
Saturn	Sun	Moon	Mars
Jupiter	Venus	Saturn	Sun
Mars	Mercury	Jupiter	Venus
Sun	Moon	Mars	Mercury
Venus	Saturn	Sun	Moon
Mercury	Jupiter	Venus	Saturn
Moon	Mars	Mercury	Jupiter
Saturn	Sun	Moon	Mars
Jupiter	Venus	Saturn	Sun
Mars	Mercury	Jupiter	Venus
Sun	Moon	Mars	Mercury
Venus	Saturn	Sun	Moon
Mercury	Jupiter	Venus	Saturn
Moon	Mars	Mercury	Jupiter
Saturn	Sun	Moon	Mars

CHAPTER

TOP TIPS

never cast spells to alter someone's own free will

never cast a spell to make someone fall in love with you

never cast a spell on or for someone without their permission

never restart a spell once you have already begun

always protect yourself before casting a spell

always use new candles and incense sticks

always end your chant with the words "so mote it be". If you want the spell to be stronger, repeat these words three times

always close your chakras down after casting a spell. You will see how to do this later in this book

a spell for
LOVE and
RELATIONSHIPS

You cannot take away anyone's free will; forcing someone to fall in love with you using a spell is a recipe for a toxic relationship that is bound to fail.

This spell sends out a call into the Universe to bring in a loving, healthy relationship with someone who is right for you, and for whom you are right.

Perform this spell on a waxing Moon, on Monday or Friday, in the hour of Venus.

To strengthen the spell, use rose petals scattered around your candle, and rose-scented incense.

Suitable deities to call for help for a love spell are Freya, Aphrodite and Kama, among others, but be mindful of what kind of relationship dynamics you want to attract.

1 Prepare a list of characteristics that are important for you to have in your partner. Concentrate on inner qualities, not physical ones.

2 Sitting in your sacred circle, light a red candle.

3 Visualize yourself standing in a meadow full of flowers. Call out to your lover, and see the bright light of their being come to you. Embrace them, and let them know you are ready for them. Release them back to where they came from, and open your eyes.

4 Say three times out loud:

"I attract the person who loves me for who I am and whom I love for who they are."

5 Give thanks to your helpers, and release the circle.

6 Fold up and place the paper with your list in front of your Goddess statue, or, if you don't have one, in front of your cup or cauldron, as these represent the Goddess, too.

Place your candle safely on your altar, and let the candle burn down completely. Once it has burned down, your spell is complete. Scatter the rose petals outside around your home.

Do not doubt that the spell worked, and your lover heard your call.

Be open to new love, and go to meet people so you can find the one you're looking for. Bear in mind, they might not be the first person you meet on the street.

Keep your eyes open for both green and red flags.

a spell to manifest
WEALTH
and attract
PROSPERITY

- **Perform** this spell on a waxing Moon, on a Thursday or Sunday, in the hour of Jupiter.

- **Strengthen** it with cinnamon incense.

- **Suitable** deities to call for help for a money spell are Lakshmi, Kuber and Zeus, among others.

1 Write a mock check to yourself with the amount of money you need.

2 Sitting in your sacred circle, light a golden or green candle.

3 Hold your check with a coin placed on it in your hands. Close your eyes and visualize yourself receiving the money you asked for. Send your intention of receiving money through your hands into the coin.

4 Say out loud:

*"If it harms none,
I receive this money
with gratitude"*

three times, then say,

"So mote it be"

all the while sending this intention
into your coin.

5 Dismiss your circle, place your candle safely on your altar, and let it burn down completely.

6 Fold up your check, and keep it in your money purse.

7 Bury the coin in earth as soon as you are able to, giving it in exchange for the success of your spell. It could be in your garden, a nearby park, or in a pot in your window. Cover it completely with earth and don't remove it.

Saying "if it harms none" is really important. You don't want to inherit money by accidentally causing a relative to die. Saying this makes sure you harm no one with your spell.

You are now ready to go and work on the mundane part: job hunting, working, advertising and selling your art, and so on.

PROTECTION
and BANISHING
NEGATIVE
ENERGIES

- **Perform** this spell on a waning or Dark Moon, on a Saturday, in the hour of Saturn.

- **Strengthen** it with sandalwood or cypress incense.

- **Suitable** deities to call for help for a protection spell are Hecate, Kali, Freya and Loki, among others.

1 Before starting, open all the windows.

2 Sitting in your circle, light a black candle.

3 In your cauldron, place a piece of charcoal, and three whole bay leaves on top. Light the charcoal, and let it burn the leaves. If you don't find charcoal, camphor works equally well to start off a fire, but it doesn't last as long as the coal, so make sure the leaves catch fire before the camphor burns out.

For an extra oomph, you could add a dry red chilli, but keep the cauldron well away from yourself, as the smoke will be very strong.

4 Hold a black crystal in your hands. Obsidian, onyx or tourmaline are all great options.

It could be a tumble stone, or
it could be attached as a pendant
to a necklace that you can wear
afterwards.

Visualize the crystal acting as a
black hole for negative energy.
It swallows everything that is
unpleasant, attracts uncleanliness
from your aura, and devours
it forever.

It leaves you clean of all harmful
energy, with your aura shiny and
strong, repelling any negative
intentions towards you.

Say out loud:

"This crystal cleanses and protects me from all negative energy"

three times, then say,

"So mote it be."

5 Wear the crystal on your neck, or wrap it in a white cloth, tie it off with a black thread, and keep it in your pocket.

6 Dismiss your circle, and walk around your home with the cauldron still smoking. This smoke sends away all unwanted energy out of the windows.

Stop in every room for a few seconds, and say:

"I cleanse this room in the name of the God and the Goddess"

– or any deity you are working with.

When you are done with each
and every room, let the charcoal
and the leaves cool down, and
then flush the ashes down the
toilet. Alternatively, you could go
outside and pour it down a drain.
Wash the cauldron thoroughly.

7 Place the candle on your altar, and
let it burn down completely.

Wash the crystal regularly with Moon
Water, leave it on a windowsill on Full
Moon nights, and if it cracks, bury it in
the ground and buy a new one.

You can use the same crystal again and again with this spell to recharge it, or you could leave out the ritual and just cleanse your home with the bay-leaf smoke.

CONCLUSION

never cast spells to cause harm to others, because the harm will come back on you three times as badly.

always remember to keep an eye on candles while they are burning and never to leave them unguarded.

remember to follow the guidelines and always to work for the good of all concerned. Do not be afraid to experiment with all the different materials that are available to you and remember to be patient and not to expect immediate results. As with everything, spellcasting takes practice, practice and more practice! Good luck!